The Hatchet Sun

poems by

Victoria Dym

Finishing Line Press
Georgetown, Kentucky

The Hatchet Sun

Copyright © 2023 by Victoria Dym
ISBN 979-8-88838-230-1 First Edition
All rights reserved under International and Pan-American Copyright Conventions. No part of this book may be reproduced in any manner whatsoever without written permission from the publisher, except in the case of brief quotations embodied in critical articles and reviews.

Thank you to the Gobioff Foundation for awarding a microgrant to launch *The Hatchet Sun* in the Tampa Bay area.

Publisher: Leah Huete de Maines
Editor: Christen Kincaid
Cover Art: Sydney Zalewski
Photographic Artwork, Chapter Divider Design: Victoria Dym
Author Photo: Kelly Paxton
Cover Design: Elizabeth Maines McCleavy

Order online: www.finishinglinepress.com
also available on amazon.com

Author inquiries and mail orders:
Finishing Line Press
P. O. Box 1626
Georgetown, Kentucky 40324
U. S. A.

Table of Contents

I
Cherub in Stone :: Animalia

I Am Here on the Map	1
What's For Lunch: Avocado Tuna Salad and Blueberry Chicken Salad, Both Over Fresh Artisanal Mixed Greens, on the Patio at Bok Towers Garden, Lake Wales	2
The Flavor of Home	3
After ~ Hurricane Irma ~ I Fly to Chicago ~ Join My Daughter ~ Attend Elsa's Wedding Together	4
Palm Trees Rustle; Mimic the Sound of an Afternoon Shower	5
The Trip Up North	6
Nostalgia Box	8
Who Will Dig the Gravedigger's Grave	9
History	10
Father's Day	11
Census	12
Living with Lizards	13
Seraphim	14
Margo's Dad	15
Mourning's Brilliance	16
Advice on Mosquito Bites and Other Irritants	17
I Hold a Near 2000-Year-Old Roman Coin Today	18
Syncope in the Milky Way	19
The Broken	20
Woman Accused of Sending Text Threats to Herself	21
Christmas Eve	22
Florida Reincarnation	23

II
Heart Leaf :: Squamata

Sirens	27
Living with Lizards III	28
Eulogy	29
let me die on the beach	30
When The Octopus Dreams	31
The Rainy Season	32
We Are Moonwalkers	33
Woman in the Dunes	34
Naming the Nude	35
The Wind Lifts the Front Door Knocker	36
In Pursuit of Loquat	37

Spring 38
I Ache When You Order Pizza in St Pete 39
Love Opus 18 for the Bassoon 40
the giant jungle of you 42
The Mower 43
How The Grieving Goes 44
Flies 45
I Can Hear My Heart Breaking.. 46
Cologne 47
Mermaids 48
Anvil and Ink 49

III
Orion on a Skateboard :: Lacertilla

Living with Lizards II... 53
Millipede from Mars 54
Swarm 55
fish flat floating dead 56
Kanga Water 57
Escape Against the Odds 58
Florida Worm Lizard 59
Possum's Pose 60
Windows, Sun 61
Florida Garden in March 62
wolf room grief light 63
Christmas 64
The Visitor 65
Palmetto Bugs Two 66
Salamander Memoir 67
I See T-Rex in the Clouds 68
Muscovy 69
Titans of the Sea 70
The Crèche 71
if ancient forest fall.. 72
The Hatchet Sun 73
I bear within me, deep 74

for Barbara ~

big-sister-like friend
keeper of bees friend
dog lover friend
lover of recipes friend
vegetarian, plant loving friend
SoHo Boutique fabric shopping friend
talk-on-the-phone, long-distance friend
all-weather friend
                white-puffy cloud friend
no white lies friend
birthdays-in-the-same-month friend
different astrological sign friend
Am I weird ... friend
Farmer's Almanac friend
I'll buy your book friend
my friend, Barbara

~ *Inch by inch, Life's a cinch; yard by yard, Life is hard* ~

*When…heat becomes the only lover to hold,
the only weight that feels familiar.*

~Sarah Kay

I

Cherub in Stone :: Animalia

After a good dinner, one can forgive anybody, even one's own relations.
   ~Oscar Wilde

I Am Here on the Map

Wednesday—between the bay laps—
and the Slow Speed sign, the one
with a Cormorant perched upon it, wings spread wide and preening.

Manatee Zone, Minimum Wake, I am here

like the horny gastropod underfoot
barnacled, algaed—on mud flats—
in shallow waters, I make my home here   eat or be eaten.

What's For Lunch: Avocado Tuna Salad and Blueberry Chicken Salad, Both Over Fresh Artisanal Mixed Greens, on the Patio at Bok Towers Garden, Lake Wales

Singing Tower: carillon bells play Beauty and the Beast, butterflies applaud. Lizard, table-height on a nearby wall gorges on beetle, beetle legs dangle. We all savor.

The Flavor of Home

Rain, rain, rain ~ grey and cloudy, dribble ~ spray like fine mold on an everything bagel.
Boots and wool, our allies against forty-five-degree nights ~ cold that makes us grimace.
This is Pittsburgh; leaves holding onto green ~ missing yellows, oranges and reds by a week.
(It was 82 yesterday) ~ the schizophrenia of seasons, the dead and buried
Cemetery walks, unkempt markers ~withering flowers, granite and marble mausoleums of grief.

Classroom of women 45 years later, hormonal shift ~an evening, experiment of endurance.
(I saved lives in High School) ~make them laugh, doctors, lawyers and me, the jester, poet, fool.
7 floor walk-up ~ nine floors from the basement garage, resting in bed beside my only child.
Sunday conversations, rain, rain ~ rainy tears ~ She is me, only better; I am her, only older.

Eat 'N Park salad bar, club crackers and rice pudding, the cinnamon slowness of Monday~
Two movies in 2 days, the hug from my nephew that pops tears, impossible gridlock ~ more rain.
Circles of water ~ the car accident on the way to the airport, water, water ~ the flavor of home.

After ~ Hurricane Irma ~ I Fly to Chicago ~ Join My Daughter ~ Attend Elsa's Wedding Together

click click clicking wheel, slightly cracked in Paris, my 60th birthday, a cadence of comfort my travelling companion—through thresholds:

lonely airports, moving sidewalks, brew pub courageousness, waiting now at Midway at my daughter's gate. Her flight delayed; my swelling feet propped on my suitcase—

everyone *searching* for something ~ someone
             everyone *thinking* of someone ~ something—

I think of the fuselage sunset, still in my eyes (how clear the air after Irma) search for my daughter, the departing crowd. We embrace like Soapberry bugs—know that in 3 days' time

we will be back here, these airport gates, clinging to end moments. We live in separate cities ~ Tampa/ Pittsburgh ~ me, in self-exile, after the divorce, on the path to retirement. She, in birthplace loyalty.

I follow her black ball cap with a golden 'P' flipped backwards—as we walk towards the terminal, the wheel clicks loudly—like me, slightly broken, yet still able to roll.

Palm Trees Rustle; Mimic the Sound of an Afternoon Shower

Umbrellas up, not against the rain, but against the sun:

    We walk along the boarded walk,

decide on peonies and dahlias in antique teapots:

centerpieces for your graduation tea, a champagne toast

    and seating charts: your friends

    your Dad, his family, your cousins,

the puzzle of celebration after divorce.

We stop to ogle, antique furniture, cookware, dresses

    (everything is closed for the holiday):

one of the mannequins has fallen, at an angle,

supported by another mannequin's hands:

    our reflection in the window heightens the imperfect,

    absurd arrangement: We continue walking,

your silhouette three steps in front; I think, *my very best work.*

The Trip Up North

Cat bats leg as I step over him, from bedroom to closet to mirror and back
nothing fits—clothes that used to fit a ghost, the ghost of fat me past
three sizes too big—three years ago Pittsburgh—northern clothes:
floor length gown, crimson Christmas party, six dollar brown pleated polyester
skirt (mini-pleated, so it looks like velvet), an actual velvet dress, green/black
that I wore to the Le Mont restaurant in Mount Washington, table with a view
anniversary, feeling bloated and unloved, we posed for a picture.

All these dark clothes—misshaped by my specter, shrouds of sorrow.
The piles on the bed:
                Goodwill   Tailor   Maybe
And then on the top shelf, the nostalgia box—Grandmother *Mama's* minks
eternally biting each other's tails, the thrift store fur scarf, black balls of rabbit
and two tee-shirts:

    1. Clown College 20th Anniversary, our graduating class
       names on the back, the fireman gag on the front
    2. Iron ore tie dye that I made at the Mount Lebo Earth Day Celebration

and two aprons:
—the one for company, antique half style, three cherry red
poppies, green stems and leaves on a white background

—and the one that was handmade, a gift, that one, for hardcore Holiday cooking
and crafting

And here's the sash from my wedding dress, hand painted, pink silk organza,
so prettily tied on the dress in the store. I'd snipped the belt loops and wrapped
and wrapped the sash around my white calla lily bouquet, fashioned a bow.
Better on the flowers than on me. Dress donated, three years ago to Goodwill.
All that remains is this frayed sash.

And here's my Master's graduation hood,
Carlow colors: purple, yellow, brown. I try it on, feel the way I felt
at the ceremony, swollen with pride and the love of words.

And then, here, at the bottom, a shadow box, the finest baby curls, a delicate frame, tissue paper—frozen in acrylic some twenty-nine years ago; here's the reason for the trip up north.

Nostalgia Box

Funny what we save—

what was important once
is just a memory of a time
that does not exist yet in the mind
So, what becomes important now
is so fleeting—delicate:

like breath, like laughter

A permanence can only come
through that which we share—those
flickering images that reflect the light—
if and only if—for an instant—bright
the cinder black interior and so do speak:

We are not alone

Who Will Dig the Gravedigger's Grave?

I remember holding his bronze urn, heavy like a murder weapon, when shaken,
there was a rattle—teeth or bones, maybe his wedding ring—felt lined bottom,

like those felt rounds on chair legs, so there would be no scarring. Forty-five
years of breathing, an eternity of cased and crated charred remains—finality.

He taught me how to sell, how to be honest and positive, how to build trust;
that in order to sell a stapler, it wasn't about extolling the features of the stapler.

It was listening to the buyer's needs and problems; it was about laughter
it was about storytelling and knowing when to close, and closing, and silence.

Like my Dad, I am a salesperson, outbound phone sales: sixty calls a day,
business to business, financial products, rapport, and closing—the other day,

I called a funeral director in Vermont; asked him how he was feeling, he replies:
Sad—I ask him why: it has been raining for weeks and it is dark, getting colder.

He tells me that he has Seasonal Affect Disorder, and he is sitting with SAD
lights on. Nobody has died for days and he is going to sniff some formaldehyde

to feel better—didn't know if he was kidding or telling the truth, his winter—
Vermont versus my Florida—I sit in silence—remember the time, walking to

Scenic Harpers Ferry overlook, where three states meet, sunny, crisp, a chilly
wind pelted me, gritty dust—kick back; a group throwing a loved one's ashes—

Huddled like we were, my brother and I, huddled in the stained-glass hallway—
cold winter, interring our father and mother—we ask the cemetery caretaker

for a moment, parents' urns already in the wall, a concealed plastic bag with
mother's dog's remains I place atop their urns, watch as marble seals the secret.

History

She poured whiskey in her coffee cup while teaching. Mother would most days either fall asleep on the couch after her final 2 cherry Manhattans of the day, which I had learned how to make for her. Or she would beat me, with a hair brush, her stiletto heel, bookend, her fist, my belt—anything that was within reach. I was often blamed, for answering the telephone (usually creditors), for talking back (*children should be seen and not heard*), for having chicken pox, for not cleaning the floor correctly.

~

The worst punishments were being thrown down the basement stairs (I thought I was going to die before landing hard on the cement floor), being thrown through a wall (there was a hole where I had been catapulted—a negative plaster ass cast, which never was repaired), and the day I had to place my hand in the car jam while Mother closed the car door (I lost my middle fingernail; it took 9 months to grow back, still is crooked to this day). When I was 13, she asked if I wanted to know the reason why I was born. She took me into her bedroom, squeaked open the nightstand drawer, and removed an old square cardboard box, with a cracked domed object inside. She explained that there was a hole in the diaphragm. I was a mistake. 2 years later, with a safety pin through the chest of my parakeet, Phoebe, I was warned, in Mother's handwriting: *Shape Up.*

~

My father died when I was 19; he was 45. My mother threw herself on top of his body and blamed herself for his cancerous end. Her drinking worsened. After college, I moved to New York. When I called her on a payphone to tell her that I was pursuing acting, she called me a slut and hung up. She threatened suicide 3 years later and I moved back to Pittsburgh.

~

There were 10 years where I did not speak to her. The family home, she allowed to go to Sheriff's sale, after abandoning it, not paying back taxes. The day after the birth of my daughter, 28 hours in labor, my Mother came to the hospital drunk. She told me that I had betrayed her. 4 years later, I watched her have a heart attack in the ER. A tumor had dislocated her shoulder. She was put on morphine. She asked me if she was going to die.

I said, *yes.*

Father's Day

This photograph:

black and white circa 1956
baby me sitting on my father's lap
his hands under my arms
thumbs on my back
forefingers on chest
firmly holding me in place
white smocked dress
dining room table
Grandma Bungie's Pittsburgh
Flemington Street, Squirrel Hill

my dad, white shirt and tie
suit jacket dark, rectangular
Bulova leather strapped wrist
handsome man, long eyelashes
receding hairline, 25

This photograph:

evidence that my father once held me as tightly
as I now hold this photo on Father's Day

Census

{I try to imagine my father at 10; I cannot. Did he wear glasses back then? He had them on, in his casket when he died at 45, thick black square rims on a corpse, eyes closed as if he had died in his sleep. He didn't die in his sleep. He had a "cancer in the early 70's, four operations in a month" kind of death—}

It lists the birthplace of both Sam and Nettie as Austria, 1894 and 1900, respectively. {They were both Jewish, from Poland and Russia respectively, or so I thought; my Bungie and Pap not sneaking across borders to meet in Austria, but, it was both sets of parents who had fled there years before their births.}

The archive proclaims Language: English. {Actually, Yiddish: mostly when they argued in front of their grandchildren.}

Genealogical Society: 005456804, NAEA Publication Number T627. {I try to imagine my Grandpa Sam talking to the Census worker, sitting in the same squeaky gossip bench from where he would *run his numbers,* gamble on horses and sports. Or maybe, he was at the hardware store, on Carson Street, South Side, where he had a store full of copper wiring and tubing, cornering the market in a wartime economy.}

NARA Microfilm Roll Number 3664, Line Number 68. {Sam pulls up in his brown Packard, small tear in the tan leather, horsehair padded backseat; it was Joe that did it, blamed it on his brother—my father. (Joe, who would eventually change his name legally to Wes Parker; both brothers, years later form a band that holds ballroom dances at The Webster Hall Hotel)}

Sheet B, Sheet Number 10. {It's Passover, and as he enters the house, he sends the boys upstairs to wash their hands, in the same way that he would teach me some 20 years later—me, standing on a literal soap box, Pap, his arms around me, Ivory Bar Soap, lather, between the fingers, over the knuckle hills, round both wrists, rinse, repeat, his large hands working the faucet.}

Living with Lizards

Like a mezuzah, the lizard stands guard,
a doorpost sentinel, reptilian Pit-Bull,
instead of parchment, a breathing soul,
portable faith, sanctifying my front portico.

the holiness of time, the holiness of place
morning's fog, laced veil, dew drop rhinestones

My father, a Jew, a mitzvah mensch sits with me,
his heart stopped beating some forty years ago;
car, parked now, in full view of the lighted entry,
for me, faith, time and place are fast fleeting.

spicebush swallowtail blurs across the trail
the holiness of the father, the holiness of the spirit

There is also a green tree frog that hides,
adhesive pads on toes, in the siding near this gecko.
They are both here for the *all-night insect buffet,*
but, this evening, they have also come for me.

Seraphim

There are birds no human's ever seen
flying above the layers of chaos, free
in the ether, golden plumes, ethereal feathers;
their songs like Brahms, Handel, Chopin.
I imagine they are there the day we meet.

I love you; you told me
before you knew my name.

In the hospital, leg broken,
a visit from an overweight brown-skinned seraph.
I smell pancakes; imagine them
slathered with butter and maple syrup.

Tell me the dream you forgot this morning,
she says flipping and cooking behind the bed.

"There are birds with golden plumes and
my leg is un-broken, and we are un-broken.
We are still living in the house on Crystal Drive;
there is warm, fresh laundry to fold."

I smell bacon.

Margo's Dad

Right before he signs/ the paperwork refusing resuscitation/ he promises the nursing home nurse/ that he will buy/ a long fancy dress/ with sequins/ if she will feed him ice chips/ He's been on a naso-gastric feeding tube/ for nearly a week/ No water allowed/ not even a wet sponge tip/ no ice chips/ and no solid food/ of course.

He is a choking risk/ after his fall/ nearly a month ago/ when they found the stones in his gallbladder/and then/ after the surgery/ the sepsis/ and now/ his 89-year-old esophagus/ won't close properly/ He pulls out the NG tube/ and before/ he is pronounced/ begs for a blueberry muffin.

Mourning's Brilliance

Inside the far corner

        nightstand drawer

black velvet pouch
satin ribbon cinched

my dead Mother's rings

diamonds   chirp

    like   sparrows'

              songs

  of mourning's

      brilliance.

Advice on Mosquito Bites and Other Irritants

Eat more garlic, they say.
Wear light colors
Use insect repellent
Stay inside.

Sleep with netting, they say.
Mosquitoes in Florida can be
as big as birds. There must be
standing water; get rid of it.

Ice the swollen bump,
Rub the bite with the inside peel
of a banana (Joey taught me this)
Use aloe vera.

Salt, aspirin ground to a paste,
toothpaste, baking soda baths,
oatmeal baths, lemon, lavender
citronella and tea tree oils

They say, your blood is sweet;
whatever you do, don't scratch
that itch. Whatever you do,
don't ever give in.

I Hold a Near 2000-Year-Old Roman Coin Today

slip it out of its clear coin sleeve,
vinyl envelope, like invisible gift wrap
land the ancient currency in my palm
no bigger than my thumbnail—laurel
wreathed emperor, mouth opened

in the most unlikely of places that sells
postcards, sunglasses and kitsch, square
foot architecture, a windowed display
case—*Louie's House of Coins*—Tarpon
Springs, Florida, across from the sponge

docks and Greek bakeries and old men
eyeing women tourists—*What's it worth?*
I ask of Louie, and we both say, "an ox"
in unison, as though the flat round piece
of metal money is readied for transaction

now between my index finger and thumb
I am transported, eight years of Latin study
to The Empire Days when humans built
for labor like Hercules could be bought for
gold; six of these silver ones, a peasant slave.

Syncope in the Milky Way

                        time is a Gregorian chant
                        like math it is man-made

but housed kinesthetically
in years, seconds, days ~

                        like global warming it is real
                        we are told to live in the moment

the false thumb of the magician
the past is the past, the future, an illusion

                        our lives, a freeze frame Selfie
                        ~ like a post on Facebook

the etchings at Lascaux ~
spin the kinescope, our stories

                        loop the loop, one foot in front
                        Orion's Arm, our hatchet sun

                        ~ we all fall down.

The Broken

The clock in the break room has a crack in its plastic face that runs diagonally from one o'clock to seven thirty-five. Even more aggravating is that it runs fast. You are always late for work; even if you are on time. The *new* TV doesn't work anymore, or the cable bill hasn't been budgeted this quarter. The *old* TV, all forty-five pounds of it, also broken, is pushed under the table where the *new* TV resides. Two giant vacuous black holes are your dining companions.

Stacked on top of each other next to the TVs are two cheap microwaves, also broken. An electronic graveyard of sorts. Not everything is broken here though: the coffeemaker brews all day, and the hot water tap delivers boiling water for tea drinkers. No matter how much you blow on it, however, that water will still burn your taste buds.

There are vending machines that go on the fritz often. Vitamin water with probiotics, iced coffee, Lipton iced tea, Gatorade, Coke, Mountain Dew, Diet, Diet, Diet. Sometimes the electronic arm that goes up and down, row by row, lights pulsating, gets stuck as the mechanics create a production of fetching your numbered drink, cradling it like the claw game; instead of a stuffed animal, your prize is a beverage. Sometimes after the drink is delivered to the receptacle, the door doesn't open. The ending to a movie or a play that doesn't satisfy.

There's the ice machine that literally pelts you, and most days is surrounded by at least two yellow caution signs with the hazard symbol and a person depicted mid-slip and fall. Coworkers sit at the broken table, sugar packets shimmied, talk about how they suspect their man is cheating on them, how drunk they got over the weekend, how they only have eighteen dollars left the day after payday.

Woman Accused of Sending Text Threats to Herself

She's in custody; her name is being withheld.
It is not clear whether she will hire an attorney or represent herself.

The raid on her apartment and the forensics on her laptop reveal a manifesto of sorts. It appears that she has engineered a revolutionary new product:

    The Paranormal Phone—speak with your deceased loved ones.

    Add the range extender to travel even further back in time to converse with historic figures from years gone by.

    Choose from these calling plans:

        Pre-historic Caveman

        Alien Invasion

        Roman Times

        Colonial Times

        The 50's

The woman is currently in solitary confinement, twenty-four-hour suicide watch, pending her bail hearing. There are rumors about a book deal; however, she is a poet.

Christmas Eve

At the airport/ my one and only/ lands/ I paparazzi the queue/ and circle, circle, circle/ a day of pampering/ like a red carpet lies ahead/ massages/ facials/ mani-pedis/ eyebrows/ beach time/ a movie/four Mother-Daughter days/ decidedly delicious/ We lunch on Pho/ return to my place/ to unpack and dress for dinner/ bed linens washed/ Myers lemon verbena/ on the pillows/ matching sleep shirts/ Christmas red/ imprinted with two gingerbread cookies/ one with a bitten off leg/ and the dialogue box/ "My left leg hurts"/ the other cookie/a lopped off ear/ dialogue box retort/ "What?"/

Dinner at Byblos/ heirloom tomatoes, basil, beets, Burrata salad/ baba ghanoush/ grilled salmon/lamb chops/ no dessert/ too full/ besides/ triple chocolate cookies/ yet to make for Santa/Sangria grins/ photos/restaurant tree/ white-lit reindeer/outside/we walk/ arm in arm/ to the car/ chill, chill, chill/ fifty degrees/Florida Christmas Eve/heated seats on/ food is love/ love is food/ Sydney asks/*Do you have a whisk?/ For the cookies?/* I use a fork/*Let me buy you a whisk/for Christmas, Mamadoo!/ Is T.J. Maxx open?/* Siri answers until nine/ It's Christmas Eve/ I shake my head no/ she bets me/ a dollar/ I raise it to five/

The store is dark/ closed at six/ two stores down/ a man/ in shadow/ facial features blackened/ ball cap black/ pulled low/ shaggy mustache/ scrappy beard/ beds down/ blankets on the/ concrete sidewalk/ backpack pillow/ Christmas Eve/

Florida Reincarnation

I am so-over-it with Sisyphus always pushing
upward—weakening like an elderly Atlas
muscles turn to fat, soft with age

I want
to be the toad, the rooster or, in the lake behind me
—the two-headed alligator

Those gulls who guffaw, in the parking lot
a tick tick ticking reminder that the sea is near,

that I can go naked into the salt water
—an animal of my *own* making

II

Heart Leaf : : Squamata

You should be kissed and often, and by someone who knows how.
  ~Margaret Mitchell

Sirens

watery Psychopomps, symphony of rain

   plunk plunk plunk

      beating on the metal chimney damper

like the bat who flew in when love ended, gargoyle on the fireplace
resting like death itself; love flies, then wounds with such unexpected blare

shrill tone moaning, not unlike those prostitutes, Greek Sirens
bird claws and wings, seductive, bodies and song, harp in C sharp

   guiding adventurers to shipwreck

      If life is a journey, so is not death?

As the wind bends trees and lightening snaps them, animals gather
outside: horses, deer, dogs and flocks and flocks of whip-poor-wills

Living with Lizards III

I carry him in the yellow watering can that I keep in the bathroom closet (where he breathed his last lizard breath, where I found him motionless, months dead). Unceremonious—I wear no bra, no makeup—finger comb my hair. His funeral, only I attend—at the garden, his final resting place. I spray water in the can; he floats upwards towards me, a small one, a teenager, paper thin—washes to the ground with a flip of the can, near the flowering Mexican thyme.

His lifeless, immature body now glistens in the light of day. I examine his claws, tail; can see his skeletal outline under his leathery skin. He had starved in the yellow watering can, desperate for food and water, crawled up in the spout and died. Was he alive at Thanksgiving, at Christmas?

In my earlier days, I may have flushed him down the toilet, like pet guppies, or goldfish, but today I minister to this departed soul who died alone. He was after all a secret roommate, a presence that breathed the same air as me. I deliver him back to the Earth. It is Sunday 5:30-ish. I am thirsty. I return to the apartment, to finish New Year's cleaning, to my cat—wonder who's next?

Eulogy

In the midst of life, we are in death. That is to say, death is coming. Everything is due—parents, children—due to die, due to expire, like milk in the fridge, canned goods in the pantry. It is clichéd to say that everything is due, it's true, even the great earth itself will, in time, become but a vast expanse of gasses, swirling reduced to microbial swarms. And even though we rehearse our death, with every fatality, and indeed, with each goodbye spoken, that slow senescence, still, grief seeps in.

He was a rescue cat, Maine Coon mix, a silent presence, always ghosting about—I named him after the graffiti artist, Mook, who signed his name to bridges and overhangs all over Pittsburgh. Mook was the second cat. Felix, the first, had witnessed my dating, marriage and baby bearing years. Mook was there for the divorce, and the moves from three bedrooms to two in Pittsburgh, to the last, one bedroom move to Florida. Always coiling around my legs or biting them, nipping me, tripping me, or clawing at me, to stop and play, to not go out, to sit down, so he could curl close for strokes and words of praise. I—always speaking to him as if he were a baby.

The totemic origins of pet-keeping started in the Stone Age, with the domestication of wolves. Our hunter-gatherer ancestors painted animals in caves—wore their skins. Buffaloes were made sacred. The buffalo dance, the myths, the stories made us one with the animals. But as we came to have dominion over beasts and grew crops in one place, society transformed, industrialized, civilized. We came to live in concrete comfortable prisons. And the pet became totemic, as in totem pole, as in a touchstone to our ancestry, a connection to our natural spirit.

Mook became the god of myself, god of my self-realization, the deification of who I am to become—sacred. In the midst of life, we are in death. A silent presence. He consecrated me to not live as ordinary, not a life of chomping on chocolate, staring at screens, standing in lines, being on escalators.

I will spare you the opera of his demise, the slow withering erosion, the tortured noises, the phone call to the scythe bearing vet—the theater of it all. When his death seeped in, I howled, drowning in it, with a chorus of, *I had to do it; it was the right thing to do, wasn't it?*

In wordlessness, there is a different kind of love.

let me die on the beach

yes, this instead of the hospital bed
bleeping clicks of the morphine drip
instead, for me, the cheeping *blicks*
of seagull chicks

let me lie on the terry cloth blanket
the one with the blue and green fish
sun & wind

let the bronzed lovers cuddle nearby
as we watch for the setting end
serene like pelicans that bob
after their afternoon fishing

bellies full, warm Gulf
bathwater baptism
green flash signals
the finale

When The Octopus Dreams

When the octopus dreams, she changes color
from light to dark, from white to brown
to camouflage, like the spotted rock coral
on which she rests.

The scientist that watches her as she sleeps,
the aquarium in the lab, speculates that
she is dreaming, perhaps, about catching a crab,
videos her, takes notes:

The Great Pacific Octopus has three hearts,
nine brains: one central brain which controls
her smaller brains in each of her arms, a complex
nervous system.

Her color changing image pops into mind as I am
driving on Hillsborough Avenue, she, sleep-dreaming
of crab in her tank, and I drive, highway hypnotized
concentrating on the road:

pedestrians, traffic signals, other cars: the steeple
of the Seminole Baptist Church, ahead, becomes
The Eiffel Tower, in my thought-soup, another
image: my daughter and I

huddled in front of the Mona Lisa, our Louvre
selfie. Am I changing color? The decaying shell
of a mobile home, no wheels, has vines growing
from its window holes,

pulls past me as I signal to turn onto 275:
lovemaking lost, by the lake, my ever-changing
underbelly, rainbow before the storm, shopping
list, bills to pay, emails to write.

Is anybody watching me? If only I had another
brain, another heart, an extra arm.

The Rainy Season

The wind pushes, cool ~ caresses my hair
drama ~ pets my face like a lover ~ delight
pushes me from behind, pushes me backwards—
a little to the left. The wind shows the undersides
of leaves, jiggles Spanish moss, wags them
like elephants' tails. The wind puffs up dark
clouds, whips them into formation, warns that
rain, delicate drops at first, then, a dense deluge
is certain.

I make it to the door. The first droplet hits my
right arm, another, on my leg. Inside, I pull the blinds
all the way up, put away groceries. Timpani boom,
so strong it skews the framed plate from Paris—
a little to the left. I run to the window. Elongated
flash ~ growl of electric, makes me smile, reminds
me of when my father taught us to fear not the storm ~
God is taking pictures with his camera; smile and
say cheese!

We Are Moonwalkers

Lightening heat July
   fields flat Florida
      flashy fireworks glow

Red   red   red
   sandy craters clay
      a lunar landscape

Weightless walking
   old fashioned talking
      naked 'neath our spacesuits

Woman in the Dunes

after the film by Hiroshi Teshigahara

I lie here naked, waiting for morning
sand clings to my skin, gets everywhere
between toes, in my ears, my navel

Sweat sticks sand to breasts, face
and buttocks, particles an eighth of
a millimeter wide echo the landscape—

a rotting romantic aesthetic of erosion
magnified salt crystals that seep in, then
avalanche—sand in the wind—a choking

burying monster.   You are climbing up
the sand dune, searching for the elusive
tiger beetle. You vanish into your own

internal sands, walk on for miles of endless
beach—sand that echoes the ripples of the
ebbing tide. You photograph, record and

artify your footprints and the sun, until
you fall into quicksand. In the stifling
desert heat, parched lips always are thirsty.

Naming the Nude

for M. A.

She was a gift. I chose her from the artist's black portfolio. I like nudes. I like being nude. Nudity is honesty. I sleep in the nude. Sometimes, I eat, even cook in the nude. I live alone. Nudity is freedom. I have sunbathed in the nude, swam in the nude, but never modeled in the nude. Nudity is art. Her body, feminine like my own, lines of thoughtfulness, thickness, fertility, curves of sensuality.

She poses, sits cross-legged, hands hidden between her thighs, leans forward. Her torso, slightly twisted, reveals her bare right buttocks, and her breasts. Unlike mine, hers are small, "A" cup, one slightly bigger, than the other, like most women. Her hair, tucked behind her ears is thick and coarse; it softly touches her broad shoulders.

She averts her eyes, looks to her right, as if to say, *Me too*. Men have ogled her, groped her, made her weep. She thinks not of them now, nor of the laundry, nor of her own artistic pursuits. For now, her job is to be silent, motionless, modelesque.

She has no name. The piece has no title. She is matted, but unframed. She sits atop the wicker laundry hamper in my bedroom. I commiserate with her, day in and day out, at bedtime and upon waking. *Good morning*! I think; Miranda? Astrid? Penelope? I try names on her like outfits. Nothing fits.

The Wind Lifts the Front Door Knocker

And I imagine you—
blue-eyed, silver-haired, you
on the other side of the front door

You stand there, waiting
rumpled shirt, two sizes too big
farmer-tanned, blue-eyed you

My stomach fills with several hundred
chrysalises, opening, as I open the door
butterflies & moths spill from my lips

Hello, I say, a mouthful of persimmon.
You stand there, silver-haired, rumpled
shirt, blue eyed, farmer-tanned, you—

I'm sorry, you say in a melodious mating
birdsong kind of way. *I know now,
after all these years, that you are the one.*

The wind lifts the front door knocker
and I imagine you—

In Pursuit of Loquat

We are both experienced gardeners, you and I
    —me being new to Florida

I ask about the loquat.

    Kumquat—you say in that correcting, questioning way.

Now, it is clear, as I pursue the loquat, you are in pursuit of me,
    admiring my bare shoulders, slightly fuzzy—soft caress
    my face ripening like the forbidden fruit much sought
    after in public markets and festivals.

I've seen videos of picking, peeling, preparing—

a departing hug that lasts too long, too close
    —your nose in my neck, loving
    the way I smell,
    your smell, grafted,
    interior black seed growing larger, darker

—we are gardeners, growers, lovers in pursuit
    of a new taste, a new sweetness—

Spring

    Pussy willow & forsythia
                    you pop into mind
                                    driving from Orlando ~ I-4
                                                  It's *our* season.
                Daylight longer ~ feather clouds
Here's the exit
                      servings of heart-shaped rice
                                  ~ Winter Garden
                                            that Thai restaurant.
              We laugh ~ Sunday evening
the park bench where we sit
                    thighs close touching
                                sunset watching, and later
                                        we make out ~ *Volvo* station wagon.

I Ache When You Order Pizza in St Pete

I want to fold *my* lips around the bump
that's on the inside of *your* lower lip—

notice *it* now, as you order the pizza   focus
on *it*—"extra cheese"   the whim of caress—
turns to ache   "mushrooms, artichokes"

                Half listening
I work *my* own tongue to *my* lower lip—
"and—two waters, lemon for her, please"

tiny booth—cavernous hunger—radiant pie

Love Opus 18 for the Bassoon

Allemande

Turning the seasons, sun to wind—fire and ice and lemon sauce, hands held high, speaking with touch. Closer in the dance, eyes are fixed, rotating earth, hairs, the leg brush. From lips to lips we feed.

Courante

Turning thoughts give way to feelings, the feet quicken. Merry lips circle and coil like snakes, both are charmed. Freed from their baskets of woe, their dance becomes jazz and wine. The actor becomes the poet, the poet, the jester. Each revel in the lightness, caterpillar to golden butterfly, turn.

Sarabande

Turning touch to meaning, finesse is intense, the slow, slow fruity kiss—cherries. Sauces thicken. The banquet line grows longer, as the moon grows stronger. Breath expands the chest. Undress is languid. First the party mask, the blemished beauty of scar—stories, pointed, yet gentle.

Giga

And now, the turn to fun—exquisite laughter, like children skipping through the fields of their everyday youth—Pleasure elixir—a slow train ride, pale blue and yellow hues, dried fruits and nuts. Turning over and over, the soft grass, like puppies at play. Breathless, our faces are numb.

Sicilienne

Turning memory when apart, smell like a fingerprint, a shirt buttoned on the pillow. A projector, film stored in the brain, a do loop, the dance, the lemon sauce, the fruit and nuts—the cocktail hangover—drunk with thought.

Bourrée

Turning to wit and witness, giddy as the sun is to rise—the abalone of shells shine. Even blinded by radiance, there are no missteps. Water is always warm and the wine, always a good year. Fire and sunset desserts. Shadows grow longer, exquisite nightwear, the mystery of the body still.

Postlude Moto Perpetuo

And now, the wind turns, passing through—graveyard fog as thick as velvet white. Chicken bones with scraps of meat, ligament and skin moan. Ravens' sudden silence, stare—headstone beckons us lie down, be still.

the giant jungle of you

after Henri Rousseau's Virgin Forest at Sunset, 1907

green grows inside/ lush and round/ buds on a succulent
laughter blooms/ organic orange/ like dopamine/ lusty tubers
setting sun red/ pungent petals/ jasmine/ geranium/ eucalyptus

I walk dizzied through the overgrown fern/ the giant jungle of you

panther crouching/ strikes/ and when I come to/ almost a year later
all I remember is/ teeth on my back/ claws digging into my shoulder
like the fumble/ football replay/ for the judges/ final decision

the gnawing/ the game/over and over/ the day we say goodbye

The Mower

after Philip Larkin

It was a baby rabbit.
No match for his
$5000 riding mower.

He'd seen the mother
earlier in the day,
—found the nest now

with the blade, hidden
in the thick underbrush:
the baby scampering

bloodied, squealing like
brake pads worn thin.
He stopped the mower,

went to the baby, bent
over her. There were two
large gashes lengthwise

like red suspenders on
her right side. The baby
squealed again, only now

staring—still, chest heaving.
Barely alive, he scooped
her up in his callused farm

hands, laid the baby under
a nearby tree for the mother
to find. He told me this after

our lovemaking that night
and with a callous face asked,
What should I have done?

How the Grieving Goes

You: swoop into me—Summer glow with nectar. I glisten.
With pollen we tangle—natural conversation, speak like lovers do.

That night, I long for your buzz—long for your pressing
kiss upon my petal flesh.   Fleeting—hurried, still—I am longing.

You sleep nearby in the sunflower—biting on—persevere.
I watch as your   abdomen   rises and falls.

Flies

You came to me, a swarm of flies...
Wave you off, I tried, but my arms tired.
You niggled and niggled and
pestered and finally surrounded me.

Our love was dangerous, unexpected...
Bat you away, I tried, but I grew wings instead.
Feasted on the dirty, carried your disease,
grew more wings. A summer table on the terrace,

I sucked on rotting carcasses and animal waste...
Swat at you, I tried, but I was hypnotized.
Circled the dumpster, prisms of light and color
until one day, the wind carried me away, forgiven.

I Can Hear My Heart Breaking...

...it sounds like tractor trailers
motorcycles, sputtering engines...

...rubber tire tread that remains...the side of the road
plastic bag, left shoe...sitting in the parking lot...

...the WAWA on Anderson Road
my stomach, like undercooked street-skewered chicken...

...I am smudged mascara, closed car windows.
130 degrees...like a child left strapped in her car seat...

Cologne

His was bitter, musty—
it hunted—followed me home
like a sick cat—
left me with a headache, watery
eyes—   taste in my mouth—
insecticide.

Mermaids

We *are* alluring—mystery and mythic beauty rivaled only by the rising and the setting sun—our melodies mesmerize, seduce you, tantalize and charm you—woo you into churning seas of jelly—make you quiver with no control, make you surrender to our beguilements—awaken you.

Matrons of enchantment, our luscious voices perk your ears while you sleep. Half-fish and bountiful breasts, we coax you with our songs. Freedom, we are, and joy and rebellion. Sultry tempests, we are, heaven notes, seaweed and clamshells. We are both one—and with nature.

I *am* like the others, combing my hair with fish bones, gazing into moonlit mirrors of ancient shipwrecks. I *know* the hearts of men, why I remain in the shadows of the ocean floor, elusive, but to only those like you. Here I am, now, fuzzy in mellow whirlpools when dawn/dusk glows.

Can you see me? I am singing to you. Red tide swirls in me. Do you hear? I am singing to you this mermaid's dream—to shed these scales, to trust my legs—to walk onto the land, upright drenched—to wrap my siren thighs with yours. *I* am singing to you. *They* are singing to you.

My voice   is the low moan
—the one that sounds a little like Diane Weist's

Anvil and Ink

Tool belt dangles, clichéd plaid shirt—He makes
house calls. It's been months since a man has
been in the house. I cringe-watch as his work boots
tread on the carpet. Ninety-one dollars per half hour,
he chit-chats about cats. His father has them—cats,
and his father paints portraits, *you have a nice home.*
And then, six minutes flat and it is done.

He smiles broadly, pulls back his shoulders, breathes
them back—I can see his muscles. I am a writer, I say,
a poet. Now, he knows for sure he's been the only man
in the house and for some time—his red hair, tanned skin
and green eyes focus on me—He steps towards me—
Your problem is 'reversed polarity'—a green light on his
yellow diagnostic phone, *Did I mention my father paints?*

III

Orion on a Skateboard :: Lacertilia

I have been a sentient, thinking animal, on this beautiful planet, and that in of itself has been an enormous privilege and adventure.
 ~Oliver Sacks

Living with Lizards II

Guess what I found? My lost glasses, I'd hoped.
No a lizard, a living lizard underneath the seat of the car!

My first flirt in Florida was lizard, lunch courtyard,
our eyes met, 90 degrees, his throat sac throbbing.

In Italy, I was known as Lizard Killer whacking
walls, ceiling, floors with a broom to chase them out.

From statue stance to full sprint at 18 miles per hour,
lizards everywhere on the stair, in my hair, under the toaster there's a tail.

Lizards gossip, so be careful of what you say,
and once I saw one on a rock with hundreds of listeners:

Monday morning, a lizard holding court, groggy from the weekend chase.

Millipede from Mars

After the dinosaurs lay down in their fossil beds and the ice ages shift from Pleistocene to Holocene, some eleven thousand years of weather ago, there walks into my apartment this millipede.

Lakeland and Venice both report the wettest month of May on recent record. With his elongated reddish body, segmented, millions of legs, slow choreographed, determined stride, he follows me around like a new puppy, while I unload the dishwasher, feed and water the cat (he climbs on the wall to observe this).

He shadows me down the hall as I do laundry, moving steadily catching my psyche; he stops in front of the printer-stand that was unpacked months ago and stacked in what seems as many pieces as he has legs.

Like him, I am balanced, slow moving, one foot in front of the other, mostly blind, a forward-thinking late bloomer. I take my direction from insects, the rain and Mars.

Swarm

for Dr. Christine Blasey Ford

krill and herring do it
wildebeest on the Serengeti

and seagulls too
safety in numbers

honeybees, and locusts, ants,
sardines and starlings swarm

peaceful and destructive
reporters, protesters, politicon

flock and crowd
throng and surge

She opens her mouth
and bees swarm out

fish flat floating dead

eagle eye, silver eye, silver floating
flat fish—Marco Island comeliness
coconut and this fish dead floating.

Red Tide, Fisherman throwback
or the eagle drop, be it
mortal hook or merciful talon?

I am left to wonder, squinting look
sun flash silver, green flash, why, why
why? Island legend, newspaper warning,

what was the year—why the Connecticut
couples on the beach that day—talk about
what?—why the husbands remain

as the two wives take their place on the
stone jetty—vanish before popped eyes—
swallowed, hurricane wave beaming.

Kanga Water

Ylang-ylang from Jamaica, distillery-plantation—
a pale orange toilet water—19th century floral
Victorian-Rococo concoction, and its second
cousin—Florida Water, dyed to a pale aqua-green.

The label: The Fountain of Youth, a woman
with a bird perched on her hand, a troubadour
playing a lute, two parakeets, two wreaths
of flowers, ornamental leaves, roses in a basket.

Old fashioned long-necked bottles that are wrapped,
sealed with silver foil and stamped with scrollwork
and a spread eagle. The botanicals: bergamot, lemon,
cloves, cinnamon, neroli, jasmine, rose water, musk,

ylang, ylang—scents set out for spirits of the dead,
ink-dyed scrying water, rituals of home protection,
spiritual cleansing, an aid to headache relief—
voodoo practitioners' cologne to draw gambling luck.

Escape Against the Odds

There were helicopters all afternoon and into the evening, sirens too. Stay at home, the national news reports, a disgruntled zoo employee in handcuffs, tranquilizer guns, blockades. Twenty-one animals in all were rescued. A Siberian tiger, giraffes and a baby giraffe, an Asian elephant and more.

The next day, after city officials tout no injuries or deaths, TV Breaking News: two four-year-old twin boys found dead in their bedroom, Highland Park, apparently strangled by a fourteen foot, one-hundred-pound python.

A snake expert is interviewed, *The African Rock Python was spooked and simply clung to whatever it landed on. The snake had made its way through the ventilation system, when the duct collapsed, and the snake fell. Pythons can sense heat, and if they are startled, they grab onto something. Their muscles run lengthwise through their bodies, so they are not very stable unless they are holding onto something.*

Florida Worm Lizard

The door is locked. It was locked on the first day of class, but the security guard, promised it would be open for the remainder of my Saturday classes. Peering into the lobby, the classroom door just steps away, I thought maybe I could see the guard, and signal to him to let me in without having to walk around the building, to get to the main door, to get to him, to open the Fletcher Avenue door. I feel the inner me telling the inner me to calm down—steps. No good for my heart, getting upset won't help to open the door—steps. *Breathe—laugh*, I tell myself, and I do, laugh out loud on exhale.

As I turn the corner, inch along the sidewalk, I spot in the distance, a crowd has gathered. They are taking pictures and speaking excitedly, squealing, and laughing. Something's on the ground. I step more lively and then slow, some people are on the sidewalk, some stand in the parking lot. One man with glasses pokes at something in a puddle.

I draw closer. Join the crowd. Still on the outer fringe, I look though the space of two onlookers. What I see, I have never seen before, a puzzlement on the pavement. It's legless, snakelike. Pale and pink, like a tourist on their first day in the sun. Wormlike, elongated, the thickness of a pencil, the man with glasses shows off its muscular body as it wraps and writhes and wriggles on the stick, quivering over the puddle. More squealing and picture taking. *What is it?* And the man with glasses who seems to know, answers the onlooker, *a Florida Worm Lizard*. Rarely seen, because they live underground in sandy soil, eat earthworms and ants. (I hear my inner self say to my inner self, *you are what you eat*). The onlooker guesses that this one has come up for oxygen due to the recent heavy rains. The man with glasses tells us to look at his eyes, *pinholes, rudimentary, reduced eyes;* it may also be blind due to its subterranean existence.

I make it to the guard through the main entrance; she opens the door. Apparently, the other guard didn't pass on the memo about the Fletcher Avenue door. As I write, "Storytelling" on the board, it hits me. When you live in the denizens of the dark, and routine becomes your only path, you become blind to the truth, to the wonderment of living, to the possibility of what's around the next corner.

Possum's Pose

Coming home later than usual, the witching hour
eye to beady eye, we hypnotize each other, stare—
tail like a rat, head like a swine, pencil-shaved face,
pointy snout. *What are you, wild creature, on my doorstep?*

I think *armadillo*. I had seen one at night scurry across the road
when I first moved to Florida, and then one dead by the side of
the road. But no, this beast is furry not plated, and bigger, sweet
faced, motherly. My heart flutters. I want a photo, so I duck

back into the car, swing all the bags to the seat, rummage
for my phone, and by the time I emerge, camera ready, over the
open car door, the possum is gone. When I reach the apartment,
the musty scent of death—I know that the possum is still near,

perhaps, in the bushes, *playing possum*. We are both nocturnal—
both actors, this animal and I, able to honor our own smallness
with a graceful bow. We employ the same strategy when we become
overwhelmed and anxious; we withdraw to cultivate the sun within.

Windows, Sun

The way I sit in these chairs—
the office, these cubicles
long rows, double screens
windows upon windows
backs to the windows
backs to the sun,

windows, sun

boxes shaped like windows,
garden boxes—the way I sit
on this sunflower garden bench
(sun sits me down)
I watch a tiny snake—
Southern Black Racer

sun, windows

slide glide the garden boxes
one to the other through
windows upon windows—
the Racer stops, kinks into coil
we watch each other
windows, windows, sun, sun

Florida Garden in March

finally, time to cut back the thyme
Mexican—it had crossed the border in
the 5X5 bed—crept silently, skillfully

two patches now, homeland in the south
and the "illegals" rooted in the north, next
to the jasmine—(blanketed in January

against the frost, and for September's Irma)
now, three days before the first day of spring
dead leaves and weeds in hand—"old man"

chives trimming, and plotting the plot—
flowering clematis between the jasmine
lavender, dill, parsley, rosemary, and basil

will fill in between the thyme—herbs for fish
and salads, stews and soups in Fall—*eggplant?
again?* (4 inches that grew into a *manufacturing* plant)

"poor man's" caviar gifted to fellow cooks
gardeners and passersby—*and tomatoes!*
caged in yellow—started early, sweet fruit—

heart of my heart—airplane overhead—two birds
—eventually everything falls *into* the garden—
ashes to ashes, dust to dust—dirt and diamonds

wolf room grief light

this room is the same—
light leaks through the blinds
horizontal lines, morning art,
the nudes, the bamboo woven
hamper, the pink chenille
dressing table chair, Millay's
The Buck In The Snow, still
on the nightstand, salt lamp
and seashells—avocado,
pumpkin, and vanilla creams
jewels and jewelry boxes,
essential oil diffuser—the
clear button that still waits
to be sewn on the floral sham—
night after night, day after
day, she lays her grief down,
a body pillow, upon the bed,
draws close the soft sheets—
a wolf who has lost her pack.

Christmas

after Clement Clarke Moore

(but then, *there arose such a clatter*)/ upstairs neighbor/ vacuums, furniture moves/ a general bang-bang banging/ her dog barks, my cat meows/ (*lively and quick*) I get up from my (*long winter's nap*)/ feed him, and (*in a twinkling*) jump back (*snug in my bed*)/ play games on the phone/ no dancing sugar plums/ I forage Facebook / Max / Celeste's dog has died/ 21 dog years, 147 human ones/ new loss to grieve/ every minute/ one less to live/

I walk a good long time/ the remedy for grief is walk/ dodge duck-doo/ serenade the Spoonbill in the pond/ paparazzi the flowering thyme and the Rose of Sharon blooms/ The life span of a female mosquito is 42-56 days/ the lifespan of a male mosquito is 10 days/ It's December/ there are no mosquitoes/ It's snowing in Pittsburgh, however/

I take my lunch to a nearby beach/ the remedy for lunch is the beach/ I position my chair for maximum warmth/ alone/ I pleasure in teeth, how they grind, tear, and pulverize/ water in the sun/ wait/ there *are* sugar plums dancing/ I / let you go/ again/ could not hold onto/ you/ a burning Phoenix/ got weary of making love to ashes/ I was in love with you/before we made love/ I am still in love with you/ but I had to let you go/ you'll never know/ just/ how much/ let love break my branches/ one by one/ O Christmas tree, O Christmas/ I can't stop loving you/ but I have to let you go/ lost love is still/ love/

The Visitor

I lift one slat of the blind to peek on a dreary day
and there he is clinging to the window,
one eye on me and one on freedom.

At first, he does not move, quite camouflaged,
brilliant green as the grass he longs for.
How did he get inside, this uninvited visitor?

Not until I speak to him to stay put and I will rescue,
does he start to pace, like a man about to propose,
or one about to run from the church.

Back and forth, the width of the window,
desperate to change glass to air, find the secret
passageway that takes him out.

I run to the kitchen, turn off the eggs, grab a plastic
lidded container, lift the blinds, and again try to reason
with the reptile.

He dive-bombs to the floor as if he knows best,
only to meet the cat who is delighted to play
hide-n-go-seek, under the table, around the chairs,

behind the curtains, until I yell, *Stop*. And they both do.
I place the food storage bowl over the visitor, slide the lid
deftly underneath. His tail hangs out. Still, the cat watches.

At the door, outside, I bend down, set him free. He looks at me.
Stockholm Syndrome daze, yellow underbelly puffing in and out.
He looks at me, then scurries to the tree, turns brown, vanishes.

Palmetto Bugs Two

I, perch on the toilet.

He scurries, at tub's edge,

behind the loofah.

I grab the tea-tree

shampoo, use it

like the butt of a rifle,

careful of certain foul

smelling irritants to eyes,

Florida species, Palmetto.

                                        I am doing dishes, kitchen

                                        sink, crying onion juice,

                                        crying over love lost.

                                        He, bobs up from the garbage

                                        disposal, antennae flailing

                                        I squirt him with dish soap

                                        push him back into darkness

                                        with the nozzle, flip the switch

                                        see things I wish I hadn't.

Salamander Memoir

A walk in Pap Pap's woods
when I am young, head down
I catch a spotted salamander,
bring him home in a shoebox.

Glass aquarium scrubbed,
I create a forest floor, a flat rock,
water in a clear Tupperware-pond
place a window screen on top.

In the morning, cage is empty,
moved, salamander gone, lost—
I blame my brother, he cries
Malamander—I think: he let him go.

Later, Dad tells his bedtime story
spotted salamander living inside
walls, eating plaster, breathing fire
growing—growing into monster.

I See T-Rex in the Clouds

massive head/ puny forearms/ long scaly tail
slightly curled at the end
he sits on ferocious haunches—
or she…

perhaps, egg laying, 68 million years ago,
like the pregnant female unearthed in Montana,
Big Sky—DNA in the medullary bone
Jurassic Park dreams

confirmed—dinosaurs *are* connected to birds,
the medullary bone/calcium white bones/eggshells
like clouds—windswept now
then muddled

opaque/ misty/ shape shifted
now—just clouds, greasy white ink spots
blocking the sun—a bobbing Bay pelican and I
the only witnesses

Muscovy

Ugly, warty garbage ducks
I watch them waddle/march,
feathered Marines, duckling recruits
clawed, webbed combat boots—
patches of red bumpy flesh
surrounding beaks, eyes and face
like some bizarre radioactive mutation
—Halloween mask in perpetuity.

They squawk and trill, they hiss,
rip through trash bags, wag their tails.
They outsize cats, squirrels and small dogs,
who keep their distance as the birds convene
between the apartment homes and lakes,
recreate a sloppy, comic version of West
Side Story, striking beaks, flapping wings
—ungainly Muscovy-Duck fight.

Titans of the Sea

after Cristina Mittermeier's photograph, Mighty Fluke

the fluke of a lone humpback, fingerprinted tail

sinks below the Coast of Antarctica, sea mist—

dusk drapes its veil of molten gold, sunset service

as frozen ships, scrape and scratch, ebb and flow, sea ice—

roar of blowhole above, a conveyor belt of water below, Pole

to Pole, below the blue line, below the salt, sea sway, sea spray—

chorus of chirps and clicks, pulses and whistles, trills, and boings

cathedral cacophony, songs of the whales, sea Doo-wop, Doo-wop—

flippers like Pterodactyls', barnacle beards, Olympic dives, hearts,

the size of three Magi, underwater pods, land-like families', sea titans—

The Crèche

Barbara says, *Florida and Palestine have similar climates—*
   (palm trees, I suppose,   and sand)
Christmas in Florida   and I'm not feeling it.

Decorations in my townhome complex are like the lights at Mon Venus,
a dirty peep show, swirls of white bulbs up the trunks of palms
Santa, like some kind of pimp, a gambling man, overdressed, flashy—
and the snowman in my neighbor's yard is a painted wooden sign, *Let it Snow.*
The last time it snowed in Tampa was January 1977, two tenths if an inch.
They fake it here—skating inside the Westfield Countryside Mall, and now
there's a new theme park, right outside Disney on I-4, *The Holy Land Experience*
—visit The Garden of Eden, Bethlehem Village, Noah's Ark—eat at Esther's
Banquet Hall, Martha's Kitchen.

(I kid you not) gourmet coffee, milk shakes and sweet treats, imported directly
from Israel at The Holy Grounds Café; they also sell bibles with their imprinted
logo as souvenirs. So, I'm in search of Christmas in Florida, hot chocolate, snow
shoveling Christmas, a stranger in a strange land, when in the distance, I see
a great light, like the North Star. I follow it to the manger.

It's a crèche, sitting on the porch, high patio table. The spotlight illuminates
a homemade diorama with a palm thatched roof. Peering in, there's Joseph with
his staff, standing and Mary kneeling on a straw floor; the manger with baby
Jesus is three times larger than the other figurines. There are two Magi, the third
wise guy is the Hulk. There's sheep and a cow, a pig and a mini-purple-haired
Troll doll.

I walk back to my undecorated home (I had thought about a seashell wreath,
or one of eucalyptus) and as I grab the handrail, look up—a large black lizard
perches at the top of the white rail. I stop to watch. He is a long tailed, long toed.
He starts to pump up and down. His gyration produces a brilliant orange
balloon-type sac underneath his throat, like a bulb on a string of Christmas
tree lights.

O Come Let Us Adore Him ….. O Come Let Us Adore Him…..
    O Come Let Us Adore Him…..

if ancient forests fall

then what of the Wood Stork, and her baby

    like wraiths floating white, just to the right

of the boardwalk, fashioned from bald cypress,

    slithering like a Burmese python through this Corkscrew preserve

—markers like gravestones naming the vanished

    (burned) to their knees, cypress logged

the language of egrets silenced, no more

    the rhythm of the pecker, the alligator's

slimy soup & salad, teeming green swamp

    gone—hiding claws and scales and bulging eyes of diamond yellow

The Hatchet Sun

How empty the lake with no water, weeds, grass and dried cattails
    where water once was
        where water hid fishes
            where water gave deer a drink

The lake lay bare, like a lover, the first glimpse unclothed
    where I am toppled by heat
        where I struggle for air
            where water once was

A lone vulture calls; I squint, raspy drawn-out hissing sound
    where birds of prey convene
        where water once was
            where carcasses now grow

Grunting, like hungry pigs or barking dogs in the distance
    where bones turn from pink to creamy yellow
        where water once was, and fishes and deer
            where the hatchet sun sets

I bear within me, deep

after Yoga Nidra with Martha

I bear within me, deep
my own ocean of swirling silence
dissolving the calcified reef of old stories

I tell myself

I am whole—gasp
draw legs to chest
curl in the cave

salt flavors silence

stalagmites, stalactites—breath—in
jellyfish, eagle—breath—out
sun, water, mountains

in darkness, the eye sees

I soar—the majesty of trees
land on my own two talons—
stand naked—wind raising hairs

a nubile shoot

Acknowledgements

"I Am Here On The Map," formerly published as "Slow Speed," *Voices from the Attic,* Vol. XXI, edited by Jan Beatty, Carlow University Press, 2015

"After ~ Hurricane Irma ~ I Fly to Chicago ~ Join My Daughter ~ Attend Elsa's Wedding Together," formerly published as "After ~ Irma," "Christmas" and "The Mower," published by Creative Loafing, finalist, top ten poems in The Creative Loafing Writing Contest, selected by Donald Morrill, Dana Professor of English, University of Tampa, February, 2018

"History," published in *Glassworks,* Rowan University, *flashglass* 2017, July & December 2017

"Father's Day," *Voices from the Attic,* Vol. XXVIII, Series Editor, Sarah Williams-Devereux, Carlow University Press, 2021

"The Flavor of Home" and "Seraphim," *Sandhill Review, Many Loves* edition, published by Saint Leo University, Gianna Russo, editor, April, 2019

"The Broken" and "When the Octopus Dreams," published online by *Rat's Ass Review,* November 2019, permanent link: http://ratsassreview.net/?page_id=3275

"Florida Reincarnation," *Sandhill Review,* Volume 22, *this is me edition,* published by Saint Leo University, Gianna Russo, editor, April, 2021

"We Are Moonwalkers," *Chasing Light, poems inspired by Burgert Brothers photographs* anthology, in conjunction with Tampa-Hillsborough County Library, edited by Gianna Russo, Yellow Jacket Press, released February, 2020

"Woman in the Dunes," published by *Terrene Magazine,* Issue Two, October 2017

"Naming the Nude," *Voices from the Attic,* Vol. XXIV, edited by Jan Beatty, Carlow University Press, 2018

"In Pursuit of Loquat," *Leaves of Loquat* anthology, Ecology Florida Press, Wendy Buffington, editor, Summer, 2016

"Living with Lizards II" and "if ancient forests fall," *Voices from the Attic*, Vol. XXII, edited by Jan Beatty, Carlow University Press, 2016

"Millipede from Mars," published by *Griffel Literary Magazine*, edited by Millica Maric and David Burke, Issue #2, December 2019, https://www.griffel.no/article/millipede-from-mars/

wolf room grief light" and "I See T-Rex in the Clouds," published by Cathexis Northwest Press, selected by C. M. Tollefson, May 2020, https://www.cathexisnorthwestpress.com/post/wolf-room-grief-light-i-see-t-rex-in-the-clouds

"The Hatchet Sun" published by Wild Roof Press, Issue 12, edited by Aaron Lelito, January 2021. https://wildroofjournal.com/issue-12-gallery-2/#VictoriaDym

"I bear within me, deep," *OLLI Connects Blog*, April 2020, https://olliconnects.org/national-poetry-month-3/

"Living with Lizards III," *OLLI Connects Blog*, online, April 2023

Photographic Artwork: "Cherub in Stone," *Lightning Key Review, This Is Me* edition, Gianna Russo, editor, April 2021. "Heart Leaf," *Sandhill Review, Many Loves* edition, published by Saint Leo University, Gianna Russo, editor, April, 2019, 1, and "Orion on a Skateboard," formerly published as, "Snail Mail" formidable woman sanctuary blog, Moon Shadow Sanctuary Press, December, 2019 https://formidablewoman.org/2019/12/16/snail-mail-by-victoria-dym/

Victoria Dym is a graduate of Ringling Brothers Barnum and Bailey Clown College with a degree in Humility, a Bachelor of Arts in Philosophy, from the University of Pittsburgh, and a Masters of Fine Arts, Creative Writing-Poetry from Carlow University. Her two poetry chapbooks, *Class Clown*, and *When the Walls Cave In* were published by Finishing Line Press in 2015 and 2018. Victoria's chapbook, *Spontaneous*, was selected by Northwest Poet Laureate Katherine Nelson-Born as the winner of the 2021 Poem-A-Day Chapbook Challenge Contest, won a cash prize, and subsequently was published by the West Florida Literary Federation in 2022.

Ms. Dym was cast by Kevin Allison for the Risk! Live Orlando storytelling show and her story, *One Shot* was selected for the podcast and published, July 2018. Her short story, *The Linzer Torte* was published in *The Scribe Magazine*, January 2020 issue.

Victoria is an improv artist, was cast in the first ever ensemble for the Countdown Improv Festival at Hillsborough Community College in Tampa, August 2022. Ms. Dym has IMDb credits as an actress in three films, *Dominick and Eugene*, *Bloodsucking Pharaohs in Pittsburgh* and *The Man with Elephant Hands*. Her IMDb credits as a co-writer include, *7 Lives of Chance*, 2013, and *The Man with Elephant Hands*, 2016.

She lives in Tampa Florida, where she hosts the Annual October Haiku Challenge, teaches poetry, storytelling, and facilitates Laughter Yoga workshops for Cano Health Wellness Centers. Victoria was the Co-Founder and Co-Facilitator of The Metanoia Retreat for Writers, Well-Being and Right Whales on Amelia Island, which happened on Earth Day weekend, 2022.

www.ingramcontent.com/pod-product-compliance
Lightning Source LLC
Chambersburg PA
CBHW042131160426
43198CB00022B/2975